I0021509

The Influencer's Impact

The Influencer's Impact

Creating Connection and Community in Today's Digital Age

Six simple steps to achieving the income, impact, and influence you want and deserve

Randy Farias & Lori Greymont

All Rights Reserved. No portion of this book may be reproduced, stored in a retrieval system, or transmitted in any form or by any means electronic, mechanical, photocopy, recording, scanning, or other-except for brief quotation in critical reviews or articles, without the prior permission of the publisher.

Published by Game Changer Publishing

ISBN: 978-1-7371654-3-9

www.PublishABestSellingBook.com

DEDICATION

Lori

I dedicate this book first and foremost to God, you are my life and light. It is through my brokenness that others can find you and I am grateful for each breath you have given me. Dad, you taught me the value of being quiet and observing, then using each word to lift up others.

Mom, you taught me to fight for what is right, no matter how hard it gets. My children, each day I am encouraged by your love, generosity, curiosity and joy. And to my best friend, Randy- thank you for pushing for us to share this message together. I am community made and so this book is dedicated to my community.

Randy

Dad, I dedicate this book to you. You said, "It doesn't matter where you start, what matters is where you finish". Everything in this book I learned from you, perseverance, determination and how to treat everyone with respect and loyalty. I love you always and forever Dad.

Read This First

Just to say thank you for buying and reading our book, we would like to give you a free 1-on-1 Strategy Consultation that will add value and that you will appreciate, 100% FREE, no strings attached!

To Schedule Your Free Consultation, Visit:
www.Destinybuildersgroup.com/strategycall/

The Influencer's Impact

Creating Connection and Community in Today's Digital Age
Six simple steps to achieving the income, impact, and
influence you want and deserve

Randy Farias & Lori Greymont

www.PublishABestSellingBook.com

Table of Contents

Introduction

THANK YOU FOR PICKING UP this book today. It's been a passion in our hearts to hopefully have a positive impact on your life. What took us seventy-five years of combined experience to learn, you're going to learn in the next few hours as you read this book.

We are going to offer a few stories that provide a little bit of background on what it is we're trying to share with you. The first story comes from a trip that we recently took to Europe. The trip was such an eye-opener that it made a positive impact, not only on us but also on our teenage children.

We traveled to Europe visiting three or four different countries and the scene was always the same. We would sit outside at a cafe. Nice weather. And around 3:30 or 4 o'clock in the afternoon, all the tables would start to fill up. As they did, we would see a table of people in their mid- 20s, and maybe another table of people in their 40s. While they would chain smoke and drink, the one thing that they all had in common, regardless of age, was that they were sitting there for hours and hours just talking with each other. The people were engaged, leaning in, laughing, and enjoying each other's company. The cafe customers would see someone familiar sit at another table, and they would immediately get up to go over for a hug and embrace. It seemed as if there were no pauses in the conversation. No lulls in the noise and the energy that they had for each other. It was truly inspirational because we don't see a lot of that here in the United States. If you go to a restaurant in the US, you might see a group of people, young kids, maybe in their 20s or 30s sitting at a table where everyone is looking at their phone. It seems like there is no interaction. Or maybe you go to another restaurant and no one is talking because the TV is blaring. But everywhere that we went in Europe it was the same scene. Whether it was a bar, or restaurant, or even at the smallest cafe, everyone was engaged with each other. Groups would sit at the table for four to six hours. They weren't rushing home, they weren't avoiding other customers by using their cell phones, or spending time in front of the television-- the people were engaged with each other. It was such a great atmosphere to be around. It reminded us of how it used to be when we were growing up.

Lori's Story

One of the jobs I had as a teenager was working in a truck stop coffee shop on the corner of town. Every morning the farmers would come in for breakfast after their chores. They would all sit around the counters, in the booths, and at the tables. You always knew what time it was, nearing 9 am when the rush would come in. The customers would all come in from different parts of town. They would order food and start talking. Talking to the people near them and then someone would eavesdrop and answer someone across the way. The energy would increase as the volume grew louder. There would be conversations that were joyful and conversations that were obviously bickering and fighting back and forth. In this Midwest community, we were Lutherans and Catholics,

Democrats and Republicans. And in this little coffee shop, they talked about everything- nothing was off-limit. But it didn't matter what side you were on when you needed something. Everyone would be talking and someone would holler out, "Hey, have you seen Joe lately?" Another might answer, "No, as a matter of fact, I was going to talk to him about his equipment yesterday and he didn't show up." Then another might say, "I heard at church his wife was taken off to the hospital ill." Then, the conversation would go something like "I'll stop by and see if he needs help with the chores or kids." The checks would get paid and a small army would head out the door to go see how they could help. It was a community of caring people, helping each other, and connecting with each other on a human level. While we love all the convenience that social media has brought us; and the ability to stay informed instantly, there is something lost without the person to person connection. We've lost the ability to connect in a physical, tangible way.

That was what we saw in the communities in Europe. As we reflected on that trip, we realized that it was that level of tangibility, connection, and community that has brought us success in our lives and businesses.

Randy's Story

Lori sponsored a table at a black-tie charitable real estate event at the Nixon Library. A friend of mine, Mike, was offered a couple of tickets to attend. He asked me if I wanted to go with him. I said yeah, and learned that Lori would be the host. My background is business development so I did some research on Lori since I was going to be sitting at her table. Lori showed up and we didn't really get a chance to talk at first. She was being asked to introduce different people to others so she was occupied networking. Finally, she returned to the table and introduced herself, and started to tell me about her background. I stopped her, and said I know who you are. The look on her face was precious. She was shocked. I shared what I had found and we talked on and off throughout the dinner. Lori continued to network and invited us to join them at the party after-the-party. Mike and I were exhausted but I made sure to share our phone numbers with Lori before leaving. She later sent me a follow-up text message and offered to help make connections for me. Her text message ended with a smiley face emoji. I asked Mike, what does this mean? My friend replied it means she likes you. The rest is history.

Lori's Side of the Story

It was so refreshing to have somebody take the time to learn about who I was before they came to sit at my table. When Randy shared that information it broke the ice and was really a great way for us to connect quickly, and because everybody likes to talk about themselves. I'm no exception. And so Randy having some background allowed us to have a conversation. Needless to say, our first conversation has continued for years.

We live in one of the greatest technologically advanced societies; with the ability to speak to a computerized "Alexa" who turns on the lights. Smart security systems that allow us to communicate with visitors at our home's front door while we travel across the county. Techy toys that monitor and dispense treats to our dogs. Self-driving cars and drone- carried fast-food delivery. With all these technological conveniences, certain things remain the same. The human desire for connection and community is as strong, if not stronger, than ever before.

Our hope for you as you read this book is that you will see ways you can continue to use the technological advancements we have- - and include human connection and community. When you do, you will have an unstoppable influence and impact.

When you're focused on helping other people; when you're focused on your influence and your impact, the income comes automatically as a byproduct.

Income should not be your focus, it's a byproduct. The 6 Steps to the Influencer's Impact will provide you an exponential return on your investment, not only with income but also with more fulfillment and happiness.

Please join our community and share your stories. We're very excited to walk you through this process and to see the greatness that happens in your life.

CHAPTER 1

Clarity-The Paradigm Shift
The Three P's

HOW MANY TIMES HAVE YOU heard it said, "go to school, get good grades so you can go to college, and get a good job?" But then what? You get a good job and build a life around work. What if you changed the paradigm and built your work life around you and what you wanted in life rather than the other way around? What would it mean for your personal fulfillment if you had the chance to pursue your passion and purpose, build relationships with people you really like to connect with, and then the income you desired was the byproduct of that fulfillment? That is the way we propose it should be done.

The first step in this whole process is to get clarity about yourself. It's a critical step to discover who you are and what you want in order to move through life in an authentic and genuine way. In the following chapter, we will explore this paradigm shift with you and help you to discover more about yourself. We encourage you to not skip this step in trying to fast track the book. If you're not authentic to yourself, the connections and community that you desire won't be fulfilling. The Influencer's Impact comes from being authentic and genuine to yourself, so take this time to discover yourself. You are worth it and you deserve it.

All too often, we're just surviving day-to-day. We stopped daydreaming somewhere along the way. We stopped learning. We stopped being curious or being excited about anything. We became numb and almost robotic in our lives. It might remind you of the movie *Groundhog Day* with Bill Murray, where each day is repeated over and over.

Murray's cantankerous character finally finds himself when he becomes a good person. Only then is he finally able to escape reliving that one day and moving on as this new and better version of himself. It allowed him to earn the love of his girlfriend and it all started with him becoming authentic and genuine.

In the same way, this journey starts by knowing who you are and being authentic and real to yourself. As you read through this chapter, take time to reflect and do the work outlined.

The Three P's

PASSION

Do you feel like you're spinning your wheels? All too often we just repeat routine habits without passion. How do your relationships feel? Do you feel empty and unfulfilled? What does your environment look like? Maybe you have messes everywhere and no energy to clean things up. What about your work? Do you hit the snooze button 2 or 3 times trying to avoid the start of your day only to be met with chaos trying to get out the door on time? When was the last time you truly felt passionate about something? What was it?

"Passion is energy. Feel the power that comes from focusing on what excites you." - Oprah Winfrey

Passion is a strong and scarcely controllable emotion. Understanding your passion is what gets you up in the morning. It is key to your purpose and power. All too often we disconnect from this part of our personality because we become too busy with tasks and checklists. We lose sight of what truly excites and motivates us.

Finding your passion is an active process that takes deliberate focus. It's a process of exploring and paying attention to how you feel and what excites you. The feeling is not just emotional but also physical. Take a moment to think of the warm sensation of butterflies you felt in your stomach when you last saw someone you were attracted to. Visualize that scene right now and feel the energy that flows through your body. That excited energy is a physical cue of passion. If it has been a while since you have connected with this energy and feeling, it has been too long! Over the next week or two to pay attention to your body's cues on things that excite you. Ask yourself the following questions and don't worry if the answers don't come immediately, the answers will come to you when you are relaxed and focused. When they do come, take the time to write them down in a journal. There are no right or wrong answers, and you may find that your answers evolve over the next few weeks. This is totally great and normal.

What are you passionate about?

What do you have strong beliefs about? What excites you?

What energizes you? What do you get lost in?

What do you do that gets you in the zone or flow?

As you work through these questions and start to write down the passions you have, there is one passion to pay particular attention to. It's what we refer to as "being in the zone or flow". This is something that you love to do, and when you do it, you lose all sense of time. You might look at the clock after what seemed to be only a few minutes to find out that hours have passed. Being in the flow or zone might be related to something that people compliment you on all the time, but you simply brush it off because it is second nature for you to do it. But, if people are complimenting you on it, it's because it's not second nature to them, only to you. Observe, listen, and feel your energy and passions over the next few weeks and make sure to write them down, record them for quiet reflection later.

Passion is the energy that attracts people with similar kinds of energy. When you're passionate and fulfilled about who you are, and what you are doing complements your passions, you will attract people with similar energy and similar passion naturally and easily. Being authentic and genuine with who you are enables you to easily attract similar people to connect with.

Lori

We do rehab houses. And at the final step, we get to stage the houses for sale. I get into the zone walking the house and feeling what each room needs. I can imagine the finished products before I have even left the house to shop. I love the creative aspect of putting it all together. I really don't like walking around the stores to find everything, but once I find them, and I am back at the house putting it all together, I feel like I am painting a masterpiece. Each layer, each texture, and color laid upon the next. I can literally spend 15 hours putting all the pieces together and not realize that it's already bedtime.

If you ask a child to write a list of 10 things they are passionate about in less than 10 seconds, they can do it. But if you ask an adult, someone who's in their 40s, 50s or 60s, you will almost always be greeted with a long pause. And why is that? Because routine has taken away our ability to dream. We abandoned daydreaming and accepted the "have to do" items of daily life. We left those visions of what we wanted to be when we were growing up behind because life knocked us down multiple times. Maybe it was the disapproval of a spouse, a parent, a friend or confidant, that turned us away from dreaming and pursuing what really excited us. Regardless of how it happened, all of that is in your past. But now is the time to design your future however you want it. So for this book, we want you to daydream again. We want you to reach deep inside yourself to the hidden place beneath the grayed-out monotony of your current life and pull out the passion to see the daylight again. So find things that you naturally enjoy doing and start making a list.

What hobbies do you enjoy?

If money was no object, what would you jump out of bed each morning to go do?

When you were a kid, what did you rush to do? What do you daydream about today?

What did you daydream about when you were a kid?

If you only had one month left to live, what would you make sure you tried?

PURPOSE

Purpose is the reason why you exist. Why are you here? What gifts or special talents do you have? Why have you gone through the many trials in your life that you have? What makes you special? While we respect each person's traditions and beliefs about the existence of God, Higher Power, or the Nature of the Universe, we do feel that each person on this earth has both a macro and micro purpose of existence, a reason for being.

On the macro-level, Author Unknown:

> *"How cool is it that the same God that created mountains and oceans and galaxies looked at you and thought the world needed one of you too?"*

On the micro-level, Carl Gustav Jung:

> *"As far as we can discern, the sole purpose of human existence is to kindle a light in the darkness of your being."*

We might try to make our purpose something grand, like a Nobel Prize level ideal. But the reality is our purpose can be as simple as what we do in our everyday connections in communities. Every event that you have experienced has created you as a one-of-a kind-person. There is no one else in this world like you. No one else. Let that sink in.

Here's an example. Think about a skill that you can do easily but your friends ask for your help all the time. You might view the skill as invaluable because it's easy for you. But the truth of the matter is that as a gift, or an ability that complements your purpose, it is also your light to the world. While it's easy for you, it's obviously not easy for your friends since they ask for your help.

Here are some questions to ask yourself to help discover your purpose.

What talents and abilities do you have? What characteristics describe you?

What are you good at?

What can people count on you for?

What are some of your other distinguishing abilities?

On the other side of the coin, the trials and pain that you've gone through are also key to your purpose. Think back to a time when you went through a difficult situation. Maybe you lost a parent. Maybe you were in a car accident or had a financial problem. Now imagine one of your close friends going through a similar problem. How would you be able to help them? How would you be able to share your advice? How to offer encouragement or give them guidance? Would you be able to make it easier? Help them to feel less lonely? Of course, you could. This is part of your purpose.

What are some of life's hardships that you have encountered? What obstacles have you had to overcome?

What wisdom could you share with a younger version of yourself?

What is one of the most embarrassing things that happened to you and how did you recover?

Randy

My friend Hayden lost his job, which, as you may know, is the same thing that happened to me. You invest so much effort and time in your career that it becomes your significance, your career becomes who you are.

Automatically, we introduce ourselves and say "Hi, my name is Randy and I am the Business Development Manager at SJREI." We define ourselves by what we do, it's our "significance". And when we lose a job or position, that part of us is taken away. I think for men it might be even more of a blow. It's a big hit. Well, my friend, Hayden, was trying to manage this change but he experienced some lows during his unemployment. Knowing what he was going through I reached out to him. And he started to talk to me about how he was feeling. And immediately I dropped what I was doing and met up with him. I told him that I understood what he was going through. I just encouraged him to change how he was communicating with people. He was using the phrases "I'm unemployed and I don't know where I'm going to go." I assured him that if he just said, "well, this is who I am. This is what I do. And I'm seeking opportunities elsewhere." This change in his mindset would help him feel more in control. He agreed that changing his mindset would help him to keep his eyes open for opportunities. I was able to help him because I went through the same situation. He knew I was being authentic and genuine when I shared my story and that is why he was willing to take my advice.

One of the six basic human needs is love and connection. We all want to feel that love. We all want to feel a connection. Our life's experiences, both good and bad, allow us to connect with people. It allows us to be "*a light in the darkness*" as what Carl Jung stated. Our purpose is to find the power in our passion and then genuinely and authentically connect with others in the world. When you open your eyes and embrace your purpose, you'll start to see a new path in your life.

PATH

Most people think of their *path* as their career or business; what position or job they do for a living. But when you know your passion and your purpose, your path becomes more about your life vision. The path of your work, profession or business, becomes just one aspect of your life vision path. It's in this last step that we create a paradigm shift from what is commonly talked about in life, "Go to school, get good grades, go to college, get a job, get married, have kids, and live a good life." This is often the advice that we hear given to children. We want you to find your *passion* and *purpose* in order to pursue your individual life vision *path*.

Find fulfillment and joy in life, be energized and excited about what you do each day and create a life vision that pulls you forward rather than having to push yourself each day.

"Where there is no vision, there is no hope" -George Washington Carver

Rather than simply let life blow you around like a leaf on the ground, we want you to create a life vision that excites you. Your life vision will define the clarity as to what you want in your life, how you want to spend your time, and who you want to influence and impact. This vision will define what's important to you regarding your family, your relationships, your hobbies, your spiritual beliefs; and yes, your job, profession, or business.

Time is one of the few resources that once it is invested, we can never get it back. Many people put more importance on money than they do on time. The problem with this thinking is that you are never promised the next day.

Having a life vision helps you make a plan for what is most important to you. To walk on the path that helps you fulfill your dreams and passions with the people that are the most important to you. When you're laying on your deathbed, you won't be saying, "I wish I would have put in more hours at work." You will talk about how much you love each person in your life. Yet, knowing this, we still center our lives around our work instead of centering our work around our relationships. This is where life vision becomes the paradigm shift. At the end of this chapter, there will be an exercise to walk you through creating your life vision. If you have taken the time to record your passions and purpose, the step of creating a life vision path will flow more easily.

Here are 3 examples of life vision statements:

#1

Health

I spend time each day engaged in activities that keep me youthful. I enjoy the social aspect of spending time in group settings.

Spiritual

I have faith that all things will work out for my own good because I focus on doing good deeds in all situations.

Family

I love my wife and tell her. I still compliment her to let her know she is beautiful, talented, wise and worthy.

I spend time with my sister and encourage her to live her life to the fullest.

I show my sister that I love her unconditionally by accepting her imperfections and by sharing my abundance with her.

Friendship

I focus weekly to make time to spend with my circle of friends. I influence and impact their lives for the better by being a good listener and by giving with no expectations. I love them unconditionally. I cultivate my circle of friends by asking, "how am I going to have fun with my friends today?"

Business

My business allows me the freedom to spend my time as I desire. I focus on leading with my values first and foremost.

My happiness is derived by giving back the knowledge and wisdom I have gained. I love to see the new generation grow in their gifts. I listen to all stakeholders with caution and trust my intuition to tell me the correct path. Because I give freely, I can ask for my worth in return compensation and people gladly pay. I use my abundance to impact the lives of my team and ask them only to do the tasks that are not in my genius zone.

Charity

I give to my local food bank weekly by setting up pick up times for extra food from local restaurants and farmer's markets. I participate in handing out the food monthly and encourage those in need with words of love.

#2

I am free. I am free to choose how I spend my day. I make time in my schedule and am deliberate to create meaningful relationships with my family and friends. I have a loving, passionate and fulfilling relationship with my spouse. I spend quality time with my children- teaching them, learning with them, exploring their passions and dreams. I see my children as fulfilled happy individuals. I love the challenge of learning, so I don't avoid taking calculated risks. I am energized by both being the center of attention (i.e. presenting from the stage) and by being alone, so I balance both needs. I am spiritually connected and enjoy daily time to meditate and learn. I spend daily time focused on my health and the health of my family. I create healthy meals and exercise daily. As a family, we explore the world and the outdoors together in various ways by traveling, hiking, mountain biking, riding ATVs, and swimming. I nurture my creative side each week by creating new things, designing better methods to do things, decorating, photography, and gardening. I travel often, sometimes by myself, but often with family and friends. I take several trips a year to foreign countries and at least one mini-vacation every other month. I am passionate about giving back by teaching people from the lessons that I have learned in life; ideas to help them overcome fears, to open their minds to positive thinking, and to move them towards thinking of freedom.

My business is a reflection of my life, by teaching and giving. I get paid to "go to lunch with people" and through coaching, mentorship, and making referrals to other people for the solutions they need. All my business and investment decisions need to allow me the freedom in my schedule to fulfill my desire to spend time with those important to me. I love sharing my abundance with others in any way I can. I have a family foundation education plan and add to it weekly. In all that I do, I am leaving a legacy of education, money, and relationships for my family. When I am gone, I want to have an impact on so many people that my children and grandchildren will lack nothing (even if what I have left is gone) because there will always be someone there to help them because of the help I gave them.

#3

Vision

Order of Importance (God, Me, Wife, Children, Parents, Family, Friends, Business, Finances)

Aspects of Vision

Needs

- Contribution – Need to serve a purpose bigger than myself.
- Variety – Like travel, challenges that need to be solved, energized by spontaneity.
- Certainty – Need the certainty of providing for my family.
- Significance – Knowing that my input makes something better by adding value.
- Growth – Need to continually learn more.
- Love/Connection – Need family connection and a connection to the history of those who lived before me.

Spiritual

- I am true to myself.

- I have an honest relationship with God where I can think more critically and creatively.
- I am open to seeing my greater purpose in all that I do.
- I have time to explore and visit other churches to feed my spirit.

Family

- I have the freedom to be there for my family in their times of need. (Physically, emotionally, financially)
- I am home in time for dinner each evening.
- Bella
  - I have an incredible relationship with my wife.
  - I tell my wife that I love her multiple times every day, and it's said with passion, not just in passing.
  - I show her I love her by giving her alone time and by helping with the boy's homework.
  - I make a commitment to go out to a movie, nice dinner, or something of her choice once a month to show her my love and appreciation.
  - I support her in helping the boys develop in their individual needs and interests.
  - We make a commitment to go away for a long weekend at least 2 times a year for just the two of us.
- John and Mark
  - I spend time with my kids teaching them from the mistakes that I've learned; however, I also realize that they are going to make mistakes on their own and I'm ok with that.
  - My relationship with my children is that of a father and disciplinarian, but also an entrusted friend.

- o My kids keep me feeling young! We are excited by common interests and hobbies.
  - o I learn what excites each child and how to help them become better versions of themselves.
  - o I encourage my children's friendship with each other.
- Elizabeth
  - o I encourage her independence but at the same time when we spend time as the whole family, I ensure that she feels accepted and included.
  - o I teach her how to build wealth on her own so that she can take the legacy that each generation has given and make it more.
- My Parents
  - o I am available to provide support for my parents (emotionally, physically and financially).
  - o I help my parents meet their social needs by coordinating outings and appointments.
- My Extended Family
  - o I am available to provide support for my family (emotionally, physically and financially).
  - o We make time on a regular basis to share a meal and stories.

Friends

- I have the freedom to be there for my friends in their times of need. (Physically, emotionally, financially).
- I have scheduled evenings or hikes with Tom every couple of weeks where we can support each other
- I have the opportunity to travel 1-2 times a year with Tom.

- I have a small group of friends who I can count on for good conversation and shared family activities.
- I have friends that love "active" recreation and that helps me stay healthy and in shape.

Health

- I make wise food choices without guilt.
- My family is active and loves outdoor activities like hiking.
- I am conscious of being healthy.
- Being healthy is about personal strength and energy.

Hobbies

- Hiking areas in Castle Rock, Half Dome, other trails
- Exploring other outdoor activities like fishing and riding bikes.
- I am rejuvenated by watching movies with my wife or documentaries by myself.
- Camping
  - Annual trip with the boys.
- Traveling
  - Multiple vacations per year with family.
- Visiting my wife's family.
- Exploring the national parks with the boys.
  - At least 2 trips per year with Tom.
  - Bringing my parents to LA to visit their friends.

No Regrets

- I take care of my family and provide financially for the next generation.

- I take regular time to capture the stories of our history and the lessons learned for future generations which I call "legacy letters".
- I lived in a foreign country for a while as a way to expose my boys to the global community.
- I have mutually beneficial relationships with my family and friends.
- I spend quality time with my family driving and exploring the United States.

Clarity is everything. To get your vision clear, download your FREE Decision Matrix today to help you start making difficult, emotionally-charged decisions with ease and confidence!

www.Destinybuildersgroup.com/decision-matrix

CHAPTER 2

Connection

"THANK YOU FOR CALLING. I am not available right now. Please leave a message. {Beep}."

Sometime in 1980, with the advent of answering machines, automatic garage doors with remotes, smaller fenced yards, and hobby computers, the isolation started to set in.

Lori

I remember when we were younger, growing up in Wisconsin, we would play outside. We could run through the back yards from one house to the next because no one had fences. We would leave the house in the morning and wouldn't return until dinner. All the neighbors knew all the kids on the block as we would play from house to house, occasionally running inside to get food or drinks.

It was such a simple time of connection and community. Whenever the phone would ring it was a fight between my brother and me on who would answer it. It was the same with someone knocking at the door. Sometime during my teenage years, I remember having an answering machine to screen the calls before we would pick it up. No one raced to the phone when it rang, nor to the door when someone knocked. Fast forward to today. If someone wants to reach me now, they typically text me. And if someone knocks on the door unexpectedly, we usually don't answer because it's a solicitation. The kids in the neighborhoods go to different schools and while we know them, it's not the same level of connection or community. It just seems like we have become isolated people, connecting on Facebook or social media instead of in-person communication.

In all things, you'll notice there's the old way and the new way. Usually, the new way is considered an improvement on the old methods, but sometimes there are unintended consequences to the new way. Each advancement mentioned in the story above provided great advancements, but in those advancements also came an opportunity for isolation.

Social sites like Facebook, LinkedIn, and Snapchat help recreate the communities we were missing because we are isolating ourselves. They even allow us to reconnect with long lost friends and family and join communities that we wouldn't have access to in a physical setting. But these sites are missing the energy that comes from real human interaction that comes from being in person, connected with people. And so when we talk about connection, we're not saying that we want to ignore the benefits of social media or technology advancements, but rather that we want to get people to get back to being present with each other, being in physical contact, being tangible, being accessible instead of hiding behind the technology.

Similar to the stories that we shared in the introduction about our observations from our trip to Europe where we saw people connecting for hours with each other. They would just sit together, have a conversation without a phone on the table or a TV blaring in the background. What we see when we go out to a restaurant now is that most of our young adults and children don't even know how to have a conversation. They go out to dinner, whether it's a date or a group of friends and everyone is looking at their phones, and astonishingly, some are even texting people at the same table, group chatting rather than using their mouths. There is no energy or connection at the table.

What we want in connection is a way for you to build solid personal and business relationships. The whole foundation of a relationship is being relatable, like working with people, understanding what their needs are. Understanding what your needs are and working together. But, sometimes you don't know where to start. In the following pages, we want to share some key points that will make it easier for you.

"People don't care how much you know until they know how much you care." - Theodore Roosevelt

BE RELATABLE

One easy way to start to build a connection is to focus on the other person. When you focus on the other person, you will be less self conscious about yourself which means you will be less nervous. Nervousness blocks your energy and makes it difficult for your authentic and true personality to shine through. So, think of questions that help you to discover what the other person needs, their wants and desires. When you find something you can relate to, say so, and ask another question like, "Tell me more?" or "How did that make you feel?" If you engage genuinely, you will find it becomes easy and effortless to have conversation and connection. Remember, everyone's favorite topic is to talk about themselves! When you focus on the other person, truly giving authentic attention, they will feel the energy that comes from being the center of attention and the connection flows. People don't care about what you know until they know you care about them. And of course, you're concerned about them. Then, if it's a good and beneficial connection, the energy flow and focus will come back to you automatically and without effort, much like a tennis match where the ball is volleyed back and forth across the court.

BE TANGIBLE

One of the words that we use in creating a connection in relationships that you'll often hear us use is to be "tangible."

Tangible, to us, means being available, responsive, and taking action.

Randy

So when you have a good relationship with somebody, whether it's personal or business, the two areas start to cross over. We had all gone out to dinner; Lori, my son, and I, with a good friend that we've been in business with for years, his name is Benjamin. We're sitting down for dinner and my son strikes up a conversation with Benjamin on how he's looking for a position as an electrician. Right away, Ben reaches for his phone and says, "I'll take care of that right now. I've got several friends." Within minutes, Ben had several replies back in regard to the steps that my son needed to take in order to apply for an electrician position with several different companies. That's a form of tangibility. I can reach out to him and he can reach back to me. In social networks, that's a valuable connection. And that's an example of making yourself accessible. It pays back dividends around and around, and over and over again.

BE EMPATHETIC

Another component that's key to creating a connection in relationships is being empathetic or being aware of what the other person is feeling or what they're going through.

Randy

Recently, one of my friends lost his job. I understand what losing a job feels like and how it can make a person feel hopeless and as if maybe you failed somewhere along the way. And so, when my friend reached out, rather than ignoring the call, I was all about it. Like, "yeah, let me come alongside you." I met up with him to listen to what's going on because I understand I'm empathetic to what he's going through. We don't have to solve problems for people. We just have to listen. And when you do that, when you make yourself available to just listen, it creates a connection that deepens the relationship and your feelings for each other.

It allows you to move to that next level and allows you to have that connection. Because now with what you've gone through, you can now understand and be empathetic to what another person is going through and share that with them. You know, we're so afraid as a society to show our weakness or our failure.

ASK FOR HELP

If you look on social media, everybody is trying to be that bright red, shiny apple that looks perfect. But the truth of the reality is what's not posted online, the actual half-ripe green apple. Everyone knows that people experience failure, pain, and loss. But for some reason, we seem to forget that reality when we scroll through the social sites and see how happy and perfect everyone's life is. Then, when we connect in person, we put on a mask to hide our imperfections. We hide our perceived inadequacies. You can connect in those areas of perceived failure and in those places where you're not perfect. It's only when you realize that everyone has a half-ripe green apple side, and if you can be authentic and genuine, you can truly connect with others with similar circumstances. Being vulnerable enough to ask for help in a relationship deepens the connection.

USE TECHNOLOGY AS A TOOL

Back in the days of the desk-top Rolodex with business cards, there was a basic business decorum where you would send handwritten thank-you notes. While sending handwritten notes would create a deeper connection, there is nothing wrong with using email or text messages to accomplish the same level of connection. For example, after lunch or meeting, sending a text message of gratitude creates a lasting impression.

"Hi Joe, it was great spending time with you today. I just wanted to follow up and thank you for spending your time with me. I look forward to getting together again soon. Thanks, Joe."

While this message example may seem short and simple, there are a couple of key components that we want to point out. First, people love to hear their own name. Remember what their favorite topic is? Themselves. Second, time is the one resource we never get back, so acknowledging that you received their valuable time in your communication shows that you understand this idea. And lastly, a tone of gratitude creates a positive impression of energy.

IN-PERSON FIRST

How many hours of screen time did you have this week? Social media takes up a lot of our time as we try to put information out that keeps us relevant and timely, to be seen as an influencer in our industry. We are spending a lot of time on marketing and consuming it. But the reality is the best and most profitable relationships are built in person.

When you're face to face and you're *"real"* that is when you really get to move your relationships on to where you know it's beneficial for both you and the other person, there's a lot of benefits. Good solid relationships, talking to somebody voice to voice, face to face, the energy that comes from being around people physically.

Lori

At a recent lunch meeting with Anton Lefteich, I shared a program with an associate that he felt would be beneficial to his business partner. He asked if I could come and share it with the two of them. Due to several conflicts, the in- person meeting was going to be postponed. In an effort to be timely, I offered to do the presentation via Zoom with video conferencing. This return text speaks volumes to the message we are trying to communicate here. "Can I be honest Lori? I'm not a fan of video chat when we can get THE REAL IMPACT of human interaction." Anton continued, "There's just no substitute for it, and I'm not in a rush. I'd rather wait and have the emotions felt in a way they're intended as I felt it when you shared the program with me. If we were out of state and it's an absolute must, that's one thing, but let's give this our best possible effort.

Fair enough?"

Connection is a vital part of our needs as humans. Making it a focus in your life will help reduce stress, reduce miscommunication that happens with texting or emails and there's usually a lot less rework or mistakes because you're able to clarify, you're listening carefully. Be deliberate to create connections with people that are genuine and authentic. Let the other person talk more by asking inquiring and deepening questions. You don't even have to talk about business, rather talk about whatever interests them. Let it kind of go their direction and learn more about them. Tell stories, connecting at vulnerability. Unlike social media, use the things that have happened in your life that may not seem so great. And always remember to be grateful for someone's time. As you focus on connection, these relationships will deepen friendships. Beyond the fulfillment you get on a personal level, your investment in this connection with the other person will exponentially grow your job position or business. For example, if your friend moves to a new employer, he will take you to the new company, but you are still the vendor of the original company too.

The image on the cover of the book depicts how your network will expand through connection. There's no cheaper lead than a referral or a repeat customer. And what better way of doing business then when you're asked to follow one person to a new area and he's willing to introduce you to possibly bigger and greater opportunities while still maintaining the current one.

Connection is key. Discover the secrets of how to cultivate connections that consistently make high returns (that last lifetimes) on your real estate investments.

Let's connect: To apply for your 1-on-1 strategy call, visit:

destinybuildersgroup.com/strategycall

CHAPTER 3

Community

MOTIVATIONAL SPEAKER JIM ROHN SAYS, "you're the average of the five people you spend the most time with. And what you want to do is make sure that those five people count." In the prior chapters, we talked about getting clarity on what is your passion, what's your purpose and what's your path.

Having that clarity helps you connect with the right people. When you connect with the right people, you start to build a community. Community is something that we all want to have; it is something we all desire.

Community is a sense of belonging with people that have shared visions, shared purposes, and you're going to have different communities that you belong to.

When you create community, it's something that makes you feel worthy. It helps you to feel like you matter to the other people and the other people matter to you. The importance of community is that it helps us to grow with ourselves and to help the other people in the community.

Lori

One of the things that I've noticed is that as one of my friends came to me in a depressed state, it turned out that she was spending a lot of time by herself and that she's spending a lot of time on social media, that she was looking and focusing on all the things that were wrong in her life.

With a little bit of conversation, I was able to encourage her to plug back into one of her communities where she found fulfillment; doing crafts and hanging out with the girls that she loved. Once she started going out, participating in that community, she decided to do some volunteer work. After a short period of time, she found that she was happier. She found greater fulfillment in her life. And she started focusing on what she was thankful for. It helped her to get out of her depression. And so community is important at her soul level because we all want to know that we have significance. We all want to know that we belong somewhere and that we matter to people. We have a purpose.

Community is a place where you feel that you belong. You feel that you matter. We can belong to many different communities. If you're a parent, other parents for the schools that your kids go to is a community. It could be a business networking community. If you're involved in real estate or a hairstylist, whatever your passions are, whatever your endeavors, you can find communities to belong to, communities that have a purpose in your life. Maybe you like to work with the homeless, and there's a group of you that go out to get food and bring it to a park to feed the homeless. That's a community.

Lori

At the beginning of this book, I shared a little bit about how I grew up in the Midwest and worked at a coffee shop. And it was a farming community. The farmers would come in every morning after chores. And it didn't matter if the people went to different churches. It didn't matter if they voted red or blue. They were all a community. And when somebody needed help, they would notice that person needed help and they would go out and help.

One of the key advantages of having community and networking is that you don't have to work as hard to get connected to other people who have similar likes, dislikes, goals, passions, purposes, and paths.

There's a saying that your "net worth is equal to your network". What that means is that when you are connected in community with people, they help to open doors for you. They help to bring you business, they help to bring you value in your life in many different ways.

One of the stories that we want to share about how community is tied to your network is how Randy was ushered in and introduced to an associate's community. He was able to make a connection and grow his community due to a woman he'd been introduced to and it started with his connection with her.

Randy

I met Nicole at a networking mixer and my services connected well with her in her business. Her line of business was environmental, indoor-outdoor air quality services.

In my business, we would use her services. Right away we started to use her company for environmental testing. And in return, she literally walked me into client's like MGM and Cosmopolitan Las Vegas. And because of those connections, I was able to take my company to a different level. She literally walked me in, introduced me to these people. I had a great meeting with them. And I remember I got a phone call from a woman from Cosmopolitan at 3 in the morning. And she just said, "You're up, pal." She explained, "We just had 36 floors flooded." Of course, we had to perform, but we wouldn't have had the opportunity without the connection and introduction to Nicole's community. From that point on, I was their "go-to" guy.

It was because of that connection, that community she walked me into that validated that I was worth a try. Her community became my community. And because of that, we ended up doing business together for a very long time.

So building community and networking is a valuable tool for growing your business, your influence, your impact. And so the question is how do you build community? It really starts back a couple of steps. First of all, you have to have clarity. You should know what your three P's are—what is your *passion*, your *purpose* and your *path* because you're going to connect on an authentic and genuine level. You need to be really clear on what that is for you.

And once you have clarity for yourself, then you spend time connecting with people by leading with value. And that is really a key piece. Once you're connecting with people, you can create a community or join existing communities. Creating a community is easy when you focus on leading with value. Similar to the story shared by Randy about needing more business. He started using Nicole's services, leading with value. In doing that, he was creating community with her. She then introduced him to the next person who needed his services. It's the law of reciprocity which is a natural extension of a genuine and authentic relationship. The actions create community.

Creating the community and networking is simply the next extension of connection. You can find the right place to belong, the right community when you have clarity about who you are. It comes back to knowing the clarity piece.

Then taking a look to see who are the five people that you spend most of the time with. If you're spending time with people who aren't in the right vision for where you want to take your life, it's time to find some new friends. If they are right where you want to be, awesome for you. But make sure you really take a look at that because who you hang out with does count. Your network is equal to your net worth so it's important that you make it count.

If you're looking to see how others in the community are planning out their personalized investment strategies, take a look below at our library of case studies where real people share real numbers.

www.Destinybuildersgroup.com/defer-tax-case-studies

CHAPTER 4

Influence and Impact

ONE OF THE THINGS WE HAD mentioned earlier in the prior chapter is that we all have a human need for significance. Another human need we have is contribution; where we want to make a difference in the lives of others. Today, in the technology world, we hear a buzzword called "influencers." In the realm of social media, influencers are typically people who have a significant following (community) and they are paid to refer products or services to their following. But, if we zoom out from the narrow definition in social media, to society as a whole, influencers are people who have a positive or negative impact on the people in their community. Truth be told, we've all been influencers before technology existed. If you are a parent of multiple children, you will know this is true. One of your children is the instigator and another is the perceived favorite. The instigator talks the favorite into asking the parents for something that is often not allowed in hopes the favorite can influence the parent's decision. In the last chapter, we talked about how we're influenced by the people that we hang around with. We are the average of the five closest people that we hang around with. This is important on a positive note and negative note. For our purpose of this book, an influencer is someone who has a positive impact on another person or community.

closest people that we hang around with. This is important on a positive note and negative note. For our purpose of this book, an influencer is someone who has a positive impact on another person or community.

In life, it's important for us to look at how we can hang around with the people that are pulling us towards our vision, pulling us in the path, in the direction that we want to go. Once we know what that path is, we want to be looking at how we can impact and influence the people that we want to be with. How can we bring them value? How can we make a difference in their lives? How can we have a strong effect on them?

Zig Ziglar has a quote that states, "you can have everything in life you want if you will just help other people get what they want."

Many times we see ambitious people chasing income as their goal in life. Grinding, 12-18 hours a day, killing themselves, sacrificing their relationships with the important people every day, working harder, not smarter, chasing the money. Some even achieve it and they are met with tragedy and lose it or are left alone with a void they thought the money would fill.

The reality is if these ambitious people took a moment to investigate what is working well for the social media influencers, they may find the key to fulfilling that void.

When you influence people, you have an impact. And when you have a positive impact, that leads to more income. It's because of your ability to connect with people plus your credibility and reputation that allows you to influence others. That influence has an impact on them. That impact fulfills the need for contribution and the by-product is an increase in income.

TRANSFER CREDIBILITY

One way to create influence and impact with your connections and your community is to pass on credibility. We heard the story earlier how, because of Nicole's influence in her community, she was able to bring Randy in and that had an impact on his business and eventually resulted in income in the same way. You can pass that onto others to have a positive impact in multiple directions.

AUTHORITY POSITIONING

Another way to create influence and impact is to create authority positioning which transfers trust and belief. Here's an example.

Randy

I went to a business mixer, invited by my business friend Ben. While I was networking, I met a young woman, Alyssa, who asked what I did and I asked what she did. Through the conversation we created a connection. She asked if I knew of anyone who could present at one of her upcoming mixers. Without hesitation, I connected her with Lori as the leading authority. Alyssa told her community about Lori.

Lori was asked to speak at the event, which did position her as the authority and she received further inquiries to speak and share on the subject.

Endorsements, speaking, writing articles, blogs, podcasts are all ways to position yourself as an authority. Having that position of authority allows us to be an influencer in a certain space. Influencers in today's digital world, promote things and bring change. It is the same thing in the real world through education, through speaking events, through training courses and even through making contact with people or just connecting and being in a relationship.

One of the key influences in many of our lives is having a coach or a mentor who helps us and moves us forward.

The coaches that I've worked with or the mentors who I've worked with all have the authority to tell me, you know, ways that I need to change, ways that I need to grow. By listening and being coachable, and looking at coaches as the authority in that position, it's allowed me to grow into a better businessperson, which has allowed me to have more impact.

THE LITTLE THINGS COUNT

If you go to a mixer, meeting, or lunch with someone, follow up on the meeting with a thank you message. It can be as simple as a text or email. If you really want to stand out, keep a small stash of personal blank cards handy and handwrite a thank you note, then either address it, mail it yourself, or have your assistant help you to get it in the mail right away. Don't be surprised when the person gets it and calls you or emails you. They're going to be shocked.

Randy

While sitting in the airport, I followed up with every business card that I received that day. I was sitting there at the airport sending them through my phone. I emailed everyone, thanking them for their time and letting them know that if they ever needed any assistance regarding what we were speaking about, we were available. So, I didn't waste time waiting to get back to the office, rather I utilized the technology to reconnect while we were still on my mind. They had my contact information and I had theirs. But, that one follow up wasn't the only thing I did. The next day at the office, we led with value by sending an email with a case study related to the topic.

Leading with value can be as easy as a case study, news article, a funny comic strip, just about anything people will appreciate. The responses are almost always, "Wow, this is great. Thank you."

ASK THE QUESTION

Another way to have influence and impact is when you're talking to people and engaging with them, ask them:

How can I be of service? How can I help you?

Are there any connections or people or introductions that I can make for You?

What is it that you need to grow your business to the next level? What can I do to help you on a personal level?

You can even take these questions to your social media presence. Put questions like this into your online marketing strategy. You may be surprised by how people reach out to you. But once they reach out, you've got to build the connection and community. The way you make an impact on people after these questions are answered is to follow through. Make those connections or deliver the promised items. Bring them into your community and let them bring you into their community. Have fun growing your influence and impact.

Start implementing what you've learned to become
an influencer with impact.

Download your FREE REI Strategy Guide here:

destinybuildersgroup.com/rei-guide

CHAPTER 5

Income

SO MANY PEOPLE FOCUS ON income as the source of their happiness and a "Holy Grail" to search for. Unfortunately, because they're chasing income, they never find the elusive happiness they seek. The reality is that income will come as a result of focusing on the influence and impact they have on the people they connect and have community with. If you take the time and the effort to create and nurture your relationships, you can work smarter, not harder. So, it's always better to focus on the influence and impact first, then income will come.

We live in a society of instant gratification. But what I'm going to tell you is that relationships are not an "Instagram moment". It takes time to build relationships by being genuinely interested in and helping other people get what they want. It takes deliberate effort and time to focus on other people in order to earn their respect. The good news is, that when you do focus your time on others, you will find that it actually takes less effort and less work to earn more money.

"You will get all you want in life if you help enough other people get what they want." - Zig Ziglar

COMMUNICATE IN PERSON

How many times have you received a text from somebody that gave you the impression that they might be angry?

Then, after spending time going back and forth by text, you eventually picked up the phone to call them only to find out that the entire time you spent was a misunderstanding.

A misunderstanding that took less than a few minutes to physically talk through. It took time and energy away from what you were working on until it was resolved. The solution was to talk to the other person, voice to voice. Once this miscommunication is resolved, you are now moving forward in your relationship with them in a positive manner. Being tangible, talking voice to voice, face to face, over an online Zoom meeting or similar types of immediate direct communication is a key to not only growing more positive relationships but also increases your productivity. It often reduces the number of misunderstandings, which reduces the amount of rework. So when you interact in person or in real life with people, you should take the opportunity to do so. While initially, a conversation may take 5 minutes this way versus 30 seconds texting, it is a process that earns a return both in efficiency and productivity short term while building a relationship that will pay off long term.

LEAD WITH VALUE

The golden rule of relationships is "always lead with value." The way to think about it is you want to "leave them with steak in the teeth." This means you give something of value that you know they want or need. By paying attention to the person's interests, both personal and business, their hobbies, wants and needs, you can easily find something to share. It can be as simple as a news article that you know they will have interest in reading or something personal like inviting their child over to your office to look at your baseball paraphernalia because you know the child is an avid sports fan. By spending time truly listening and connecting, you will find ways to add value. If you do this in an authentic and genuine manner, the recipient will want to reciprocate value back to you.

This is where you will start to see the return on your investment in relationships increase financially.

START SMALL AND THINK BIG

"Whoever can be trusted with very little can also be trusted with much, and whoever is dishonest with very little will also be dishonest with much"
-The Bible, Luke 16:10

It's common to think about getting a big contract with the whale client when you first meet them, but again, respect is not given, it's earned. So you need both time and consistency to earn the client's respect where they will hand you the big contract. The good news is that earning trust starts with simple things. For example, let's say you are having lunch with a client and they ask you for something. You say, "yes, I will get back to you tomorrow on that." You now have a chance to prove to them that you are reliable and responsible. The key is to get back to them when you said you would. Unfortunately, we see people make a commitment to someone, and then days go by. They don't call because they don't have the answer yet. Then, finally, they get the answer and call back only to be sent to voicemail and the client ghosts them. The correct action would have been to call them back, as promised, even if to say that you needed to recommit to another time in order to get the answer.

HONOR YOUR WORD

Your word is your value. So, once you start delivering on the small things on time, they will start to use you and test you with smaller projects. Don't think that it's not worth your time. You might think you really don't want to do that smaller job or you really don't want to give away your golden nugget for nothing. But you know what? Once you do, they will come back for more. They will look to you for bigger jobs or contracts. They most likely will even trust you to help them with personal business needs or ask for referrals that you know because they want to be with more people like you. So, it's all about creating relationships first, putting the clients first and. listening to what their needs and wants are when you do that consistently, then you will start to create long term value.

Here is a story about how an associate of Randy's didn't listen to the needs of Randy's client, but rather he tried to push his own agenda which resulted in losing the recurring revenues of a lifetime client.

Mr. and Mrs. Bethany owned a lot of properties; houses and commercial property rentals. I had worked with them for many years, helping them with service needs when it came to their shopping centers and restaurants and their rental properties. They had a tenant that was a long-term tenant who was taking care of their property. Mr. and Mrs. Bethany wanted to put new carpet in her place, but they wanted something a little nicer than apartment grade carpet. I met with them and we talked it through, but I was leaving town on vacation. I left instructions with my colleague that Mr. and Mrs. Bethany were going to come into the storefront to pick out the carpet and I told him the carpet grade we had settled on. They were coming in to purchase the carpet and schedule it to get installed. I know I made myself clear to my colleague, but when I got back and made the phone call to Mr. Bethany to see how everything went, he was literally upset to the point where I lost him as a client. My colleague spent time trying to sell him on something different than what we had talked about because we had that in inventory and he wanted to unload it. But it's not what Mr. and Mrs. Bethany wanted and after expressing that several times to my colleague, they left without making a purchase and they didn't come back as a client. So, it's important that the line of communication throughout your relationships are very clear. It's important. I lost a valuable client. And not only that but those clients had been good to me. They were good people. They were great clients. And the whole episode was a painful, but valuable life lesson that I'll never forget.

EARN RESPECT OVER TIME

There's a saying, "respect is not given. It's earned." So short term relationships can turn into long term relationships if you take the time to invest in the relationship. Take a little time to determine the value of what your client is worth as one transaction and then what the value of a lifetime client is. The most expensive client is the new client; the cheapest client is a return client. So, if you focus on a relationship rather than the income, you can grow your income with fewer costs and effort. For example, as we shared in the story, Mr. and Mrs. Bethany not only had the one rental they were replacing carpet on, they had many other properties that we lost the opportunity to serve because of a short term vision that the associate had instead of listening to what the client wanted. So in creating relationships, it's key to listen to the client, to look at how you can make a positive impact on the client's life.

GIVE THEN ASK

Another story about leading with value comes from an associate. This story shows how you can ask for what you need after you lead with value. He was assisting his dad, who was a renowned scientist, to share a book that was written for the general public. He was working to get his dad booked on various podcasts and radio shows with influencers in these markets. One key influencer had an interest in a topic our associate's dad was well versed in. Rather than approaching this influencer with a pitch on why he should put his dad on his podcast, my associate led with value. He researched the influencer enough to know he had a great interest in the exact field our associate's father was an expert in. So, when he had an opportunity, he led with an introduction to his father. Within a short period of time, our associate asked for some airtime to pitch his dad's book. It was a "no brainer" for the influencer to host his father on his podcast after he received value.

BE DELIBERATE

"If you fail to plan, you plan to fail." One of the things that we suggest is to be deliberate on your calendar and book time blocks to focus on face to face with people, book time to make phone calls, voice to voice. Once you have those time blocks in your calendar, you can focus on other things like reviewing emails, making social media posts, etc. Once the time is spent, you never get it back, so it is critical to put the important interactions such as these meetings into your calendar so they actually happen. The return on investment that you get being in front of people, talking to people will far outweigh any of the other tasks that you have on your list.

Additionally, what you'll find is that often these business relationships turn into personal relationships too. And why wouldn't it? If you did the work of the *Three P's* and you have clarity around your purpose, you will be connecting with people who have similar energy and interests as you. When you show that you are trustworthy, reliable and responsible, they will want to connect at an even more intimate and personal level. Many times, when we're doing business with someone, we'll hear of a need that they have outside of the business. We reach out to help them and this action starts to create fulfillment for us. But it also creates a lifetime client, because now the client looks at you as a friend. When you are connected on a personal level, that lifetime value of that client grows exponentially because now when they move to a different position or company, they take you along, but the original position now has a new person who will call you because you are on the shortlist.

This is why we want you to focus on the relationships, not the income. When you use your influence to create positive impacts on people, you will feel fulfilled, but the value will be returned to you exponentially. It's going to expand your business. There's nothing cheaper than repeat business or referral business. That's what you're creating when you create these relationships. But the caveat is you can't create them in a contrived method. You need to be authentic and genuine. Remember, the quote that if you help enough people get what they want, you'll get what you want. When you have the heart to do that, nothing can stop you.

We are talking about helping our business clients get what they want, focusing on spending time with those most important people, so helping them also follows these same rules. People are people. Take the time to time block your calendar to be deliberate and spend time with those you love and care for. If you take the time to find out how to help those who are important to you, you will build deeper connections with those you care about. In being attentive to their needs and their wants, you'll get what you want.

The bottom line of what we're trying to get to in this book is when you focus on people and relationships, you will get a return on your investment that is both in the form of financial rewards and life fulfillment.

Because we want you to make the best financial decisions, we're offering you a FREE Tax Strategy Consultation with Lori so you can explore your tax exposure on capital gains BEFORE you sell. It's about what you keep more than what you make.

Schedule Your FREE Tax Strategy Consultation Here:

www.Destinybuildersgroup.com/tax-calculator/

CHAPTER 6

The Roadmap to Success...
Pulling it all Together

WHAT DOES THE ROAD MAP TO success really look like? In this book, so far we have discussed six steps, the six simple steps to achieving income, impact, and influence. If you remember, we started out with the *Three P's*, which are our *passion, purpose, and path*. The *Three P's* are the key starting point because when you understand yourself enough to be genuine and authentic, you will connect and have a community that flows with ease naturally. Understanding that passion is energy and it's what excites and makes it much easier and much more natural to move forward to find your purpose. Then, effortlessly and almost automatically, your path will unfold before you. This clarity is so key because it leads to a genuine and authentic connection. When you are authentically connecting with people, genuinely caring about them, it's going to lead to community and those communities are going to lead you to have more influence and impact, which leads to income.

While it might seem that this is the longer path to make the income, the return on your time and your authentic connection actually give you an exponential return. You will make so much more on all fronts, fulfillment, personal satisfaction, happiness, and income. This is the

Influencer's Impact, which is why we chose to write this book. And it's the story of how we live.

Randy

I'm the kind of guy who wears my heart on my sleeve. I can't change that. That's who I am. But because I care about people and I want to help people. I reached out to one of our contractors who we have a great relationship with; I really like this guy. I see him wanting to do more in his business, but not sure how to navigate through this process. Most technicians don't have the experience needed to grow their business by themselves. I connect with him because he's real. So I had lunch with him yesterday where we took the time to talk and get to know each other more. I asked him how can I help him get to where he wants to get to? The result is that we formed an informal partnership.

And because of the informal partnership, I can introduce him to my circles to obtain more business for him and he will pay referrals to me. He's our guy in the field and we could have left it at that, but I live by the mantra of leading with value. I can help him, focus on him and because of my influence and impact, the income will come.

Another evening, we had another gentleman come over to get paid. About an hour later after paying him, he's knocking at the door and he's giving us homemade food. He brought us dinner unexpectedly. He led with value back to us. That's joy, a relationship that we benefit from on multiple levels. I know that I can call any of these guys at any given moment and they will drop anything for me because I would do the same thing for them. You know the impact and influence, it's so important.

We want you to change your paradigm. We want you to build your life first and then fit your job, your profession or your business into it. And when you do that, you're no longer chasing the money. You're chasing your impact and influence. The money comes.

By doing that, you have more control of your life, more control of your current situation, more fulfillment, more gratitude. You end up living your best life, which is what we're doing. We live a life of passion and purpose. We live a life of connection and community. We live a life of Influence and Impact. That is our purpose and passion. So, when you really get clear on what it is you want and you create that path for yourself and you focus on connecting with people, the door opens automatically to the income. It is just amazing to us all the opportunities that come our way. The relationships that we have. We feel so fulfilled and so grateful for everything that we have because we focus on the relationship between people.

So, in conclusion, our hope for you is that you too can get to this point of living with clarity, connection, and community. I know that sometimes life feels like the movie *Groundhog Day*. You are just doing the same thing day in, day out. You are not feeling fulfilled. You are not feeling like you will ever catch up. You feel like you're always reaching but never achieving what you want or that you're just surviving, not thriving. Our hope is that after reading this book, you'll have some inspiration to bring joy back into your life.

We want to share this final quote with you. The author is unknown and we hope that it resonates with you.

"You might think that you don't matter in this world, but someone hears a song on the radio and it reminds them of you. Someone has read a book that you recommended to them and gotten lost in its pages. Someone has remembered a joke that you told them and smiled to themselves. Never think that you don't have an impact. Your fingerprints can't be wiped away from the little marks of kindness that you've left behind."

Let us help you map out your success.

Apply to set up a 1-on-1 strategy call here:

www.Destinybuildersgroup.com/strategycall/

Read This First

Just to say thank you for buying and reading our book, we would like to give you a free 1-on-1 Strategy Consultation that will add value and that you will appreciate, 100% FREE, no strings attached!

To Schedule Your Free Consultation, Visit:
www.Destinybuildersgroup.com/strategycall/

I appreciate your interest in my book, and I value your feedback as it helps me improve future versions of this book. I would appreciate it if you could leave your invaluable review on Amazon.com with your feedback. Thank you!

www.ingramcontent.com/pod-product-compliance
Lightning Source LLC
Chambersburg PA
CBHW061049050326
40690CB00012B/2563